TV COOKS

Madhur Jaffrey

COOKS

Curries

Photographs by Philip Webb

Published by BBC Books,
an imprint of BBC Worldwide Publishing.
BBC Worldwide Limited, Woodlands,
80 Wood Lane, London W12 0TT.

The recipes in this book first appeared in the following:

Madhur Jaffrey's Far Eastern Cookery
©Madhur Jaffrey, 1989

Madhur Jaffrey's Illustrated Indian Cookery
©Madhur Jaffrey, 1982

Madhur Jaffrey's Indian Cookery
©Madhur Jaffrey, 1982

Madhur Jaffrey's Quick & Easy Indian Cookery
©Madhur Jaffrey, 1993

This edition first published 1996
© Madhur Jaffrey1996
The moral right of the author
has been asserted

ISBN 0 563 38794 7

Edited by Pam Mallender
Designed by DW Design
Photographs by Philip Webb
Styling by Helen Payne
Home Economist Caroline Liddle

Set in New Caledonia and Helvetica
Printed and bound in Belgium by Proost NV
Colour separations by Colour Origination Ltd, London
Cover printed by Proost NV

Cover and frontispiece: Stir-fried Prawns in an Aromatic
Tomato-Cream Sauce.

CONTENTS

RECIPE NOTES

Eggs are size 2.
Wash all fresh produce before preparation and peel as necessary.
Spoon measurements are level. Always use proper measuring spoons:
1 teaspoon = 5ml and 1 tablespoon = 15ml.
Never mix metric or imperial measures in one recipe. Stick to one or the other.
Whole spices included in recipes are not meant to be eaten.

HANDY CONVERSION TABLES

Weight		Volume		Linear	
15g	½oz	30ml	1fl oz	5mm	⅛in
25g	1oz	50ml	2fl oz	10mm/1cm	½in
40g	1½oz	100ml	3½fl oz	2cm	¾in
55g	2oz	125ml	4fl oz	2.5cm	1in
85g	3oz	150ml	5fl oz (¼ pint)	5cm	2in
115g	4oz	175ml	6fl oz	7.5cm	3in
140g	5oz	200ml	7fl oz (⅓ pint)	10cm	4in
175g	6oz	225ml	8fl oz	13cm	5in
200g	7oz	250ml	9fl oz	15cm	6in
225g	8oz	300ml	10fl oz (½ pint)	18cm	7in
250g	9oz	350ml	12fl oz	20cm	8in
280g	10oz	400ml	14fl oz	23cm	9in
350g	12oz	425ml	15fl oz (¾ pint)	25cm	10in
375g	13oz	450ml	16fl oz	28cm	11in
400g	14oz	500ml	18fl oz	30cm	12in
425g	15oz	600ml	20fl oz (1 pint)		
450g	1lb	700ml	1¼ pints		
550g	1¼lb	850ml	1½ pints		
750g	1lb 10oz	1 litre	1¾ pints		
900g	2lb	1.2 litres	2 pints		
1kg	2¼lb	1.3 litres	2¼ pints		
1.3kg	3lb	1.4 litres	2½ pints		
1.8kg	4lb	1.7 litres	3 pints		
2.25kg	5lb	2 litres	3½ pints		
		2.5 litres	4½ pints		

Oven temperatures

225F	110C	GAS ¼
250F	120C	GAS ½
275F	140C	GAS 1
300F	150C	GAS 2
325F	160C	GAS 3
350F	180C	GAS 4
375F	190C	GAS 5
400F	200C	GAS 6
425F	220C	GAS 7
450F	230C	GAS 8
475F	240C	GAS 9

SERVING NOTES

Generally, an Indian meal consists of a meat dish, a vegetable dish, bread and/or rice, a pulse dish, a yogurt relish and a fresh chutney or small, relish-like salad. Fruit is served at the end of the meal. Sometimes when the meat dish is particularly rich, the pulse dish is eliminated and a pullao rice is served. Vegetarians increase the number of vegetable and pulse dishes. Most Indians like to use their right hands to eat, using bread to scoop up meat or vegetables. Most foods are put beside each other on plates. Very wet dishes meant to be eaten with bread are served in small individual bowls or are sometimes ladled on top of the rice.

 Suitable for vegetarians   **Suitable for freezing**

Indians use spices and seasonings like masterful magicians, putting just the right amount of ginger, coriander or cumin into the pot at just the right time to produce aromatic, pungently-flavoured dishes of lamb, chicken, fish, eggs and vegetables. All that is left to be done then is to devour them with some gleaming white rice or perhaps a naan or two.

The purpose of this book is to show you how you too can make these curries, some from India and others from Thailand, Indonesia and Malaysia – countries where Indians migrated, traded or otherwise left their mark. Many of the dishes in the book are very simple to prepare. All that the Curried Tuna requires is some onion, garlic, ginger, curry powder and a can of tuna. I take this on picnics or have it on toast for a quick lunch. Then there is the Quick Chicken Korma: heat some oil, watch the cinnamon sticks uncurl and the cardomom pods stiffen, put in some ginger, garlic, onion and tomato and finally the chicken.

If you want an elaborate Indian meal, there are Chick Peas Cooked in Tea, Red Lentils 'Tarka', Mushroom Curry, Cabbage Stir-Fried with Red Pepper Paste and all manner of chutneys and relishes to complement the meat and fish curries.

You will find this to be a handy little book, ready to satisfy that craving for magically spiced foods.

INGREDIENTS

Asafoetida
This brownish resin of strong odour (it has been compared to the smell of very strong truffles) is used to give a special 'kick' to Indian foods. It comes from a 3m/10ft high plant – a type of fennel – the milky sap of which solidifies into this pale rust-brown resin which darkens with age. It is used in very small quantities and subtly transforms the taste of a dish. For easy use, buy the ground variety which can be found at Indian and Pakistani grocers. Make sure the lid sits tightly on the box when you store it. It is also a digestive.

Chillies
Fresh hot green and red: red chillies are just ripe green chillies, their flavour is slightly different though but their intensity can be exactly the same. If you cannot find fresh red chillies, a combination of the common sweet red pepper with paprika and chilli powder makes the best substitute. Chillies vary tremendously in size, shape and heat and it might take a little experimenting to find those you like best. To store fresh chillies, wrap in newspaper, then plastic and keep in the fridge. They should last for several weeks. Any that begin to soften and rot should be removed as they tend to infect the whole batch. Chillies can also be washed, dried and then frozen whole in plastic containers.
Dried hot red chillies: these are normally 4-5cm/1½-2in long and 1cm/½in wide and are often thrown into hot oil for a few seconds until they puff up and their skin darkens. This fried skin adds its own very special flavour to a host of meats, vegetables and pulses. If you want the flavour without the heat, make a small opening in them and shake out and discard their seeds. When used for making a spice paste they are usually soaked in water before being ground with other spices.

Cinnamon
This is the inner bark of a small evergreen tree native to Sri Lanka. It is a popular spice with a sweet, pungent flavour. Buy sticks which are used for their flavour and aroma and are not meant to be eaten.

Coconut milk
Sometimes because of the fat contained in canned coconut milk it tends to become very grainy. To rectify, either process in a blender for a few seconds or beat well. Canned coconut milk, which should be creamy white and not oily, is best added towards the end of cooking time. Care must be taken it does not curdle – stir constantly as it cooks. Once opened, coconut milk doesn't keep well. Even kept in the fridge it generally does not last for more than a few days.

Coriander seeds
Coriander seeds have a mild, sweet, orangey flavour and are sold whole or ground. They are the round, beige seeds of the coriander plant and in their ground form one of India's most common and cheapest spices. Buy small quantitites, ground coriander begins to taste like sawdust after several months. Grind whole coriander seeds in a coffee grinder, then put through a sieve if you need ground coriander.

Galangal
This ginger-like rhizome has a very distinct earthy aroma of its own and a mildly peppery ginger flavour. There are two varieties, greater (laos) and lesser (kenchur), the lesser having the more intensely spicy flavour. It can be found as a fresh root, a dried root, which has to be soaked before use, and ground (labelled Laos powder).

Lemon grass
This has thick, grass-like leaves which smell and taste strongly of lemon. Store fresh lemon grass with its bottom end in a little water to prevent it from drying out, or freeze. The best equivalent is lemon rind, though it is nowhere near as good as the real thing.

Tamarind paste

Tamarind is the bean-like fruit of a tall tree. It is dark brown and slightly sticky with an acidic taste that is very refreshing. It is usually sold in a compacted or dried form. To make the paste: break off 225g/8oz and tear into small pieces, place in a bowl and pour over 450ml/16fl oz very hot water and leave for 3 hours or overnight. (You can achieve the same result by simmering for 10 minutes.) Press through a sieve, place what tamarind remains back into the bowl and pour over 125ml/4fl oz of hot water, mash then push through the sieve. This will make about 350ml/12fl oz of paste. It will keep in the fridge for two to three weeks, or it can be frozen.

EQUIPMENT

Blenders and food processors

In India, grinding stones, which consist of a large flat stone that just sits and a smaller stone moved manually on top which does the actual grinding, are used for grinding garlic, onions and ginger. These stones are exceedingly heavy and no longer essential. Their place can be taken by food processors and blenders. When buying a blender make sure that its blades sit close to the bottom, so it can pulverise small quantities adequately.

Coffee grinder

Dry spices cannot be ground in blenders or food processors – only a coffee grinder will do. Just wipe it out with a dry or very lightly dampened cloth when you are finished. I keep an extra one especially for the purpose.

Electric rice cooker

This can be a useful piece of equipment. It has a large covered pan which sits on top of an electric element. When the water has been absorbed by the rice, the cooker switches itself off.

Ginger grater

The Japenese make a special grater for ginger and horseradish. It has no holes or openings but tiny hair-like spikes that grates ginger to a pulp in seconds. What is best, it holds the rough fibres back while allowing me to collect the pulp. You can use the finest part of an ordinary grater.

Karhai

This is very similar to a Chinese wok. If you took a large, hollow ball and cut it into half, that would be about the shape of a karhai. I'm not suggesting you buy one, but it is excellent for deep-frying and stir frying.

Pans

Cast-iron: I find a 13cm/5in cast-iron frying pan ideal for roasting spices – it can be heated without oil or water in it – and for frying small amounts of spices in oil. A larger one is useful if you are making Indian breads such as parathas and chapatis. Once properly seasoned they should never be scrubbed with abrasive cleaners. Non-stick: these take the worry out of cooking many foods. The heavier the pan, the better its quality usually is. Browning meats do not stick to the bottom, nor do sauces with ginger and almonds. They are best used with plastic or wooden utensils that will not scratch the surface.

Tongs

These come in handy when you need to turn pieces of meat or when you need to delve into a sauce to remove, say, a bay leaf. Make sure they move easily before buying. Stiff tongs are virtually useless.

1	Dried red chillies
2	Galangal
3	Fresh coriander
4	Red lentils
5	Cumin seeds
6	Fresh root ginger
7	Okra
8	Fresh red and green chillies
9	Mustard seeds
10	Cardamom pods
11	Dried black-eyed beans
12	Canned chick peas
13	Long grain rice
14	Basmati rice
15	Lemon grass
16	Fennel seeds
17	Cinnamon sticks
18	Whole cloves
19	Asafoetida
20	Kaffir lime leaves
21	Curry leaves
22	Squid
23	Scallops
24	Chana dal
25	Yellow split peas
26	Raw prawns
27	Canned coconut milk

1. Karhai

2. Stainless-steel frying pan and lid

3. Tongs

4. Cooking utensils

5. Ginger grater

6. Rice cooker

7. Coffee grinder

8. Pestle and mortar

9. Blender

Meat

THAI PORK CURRY IN THE BURMESE STYLE
(KAENG HUNGLAY) ⊛

Those familiar with India's hot, sweet and sour vindaloo will find that this is almost a sister curry. After all, Burma borders India and the ripple effect of cultural exchanges can be quite far-reaching.

Serves 4–6

800g boneless pork cut into 4cm/1½in cubes (See Tip)

1½ tbsp Japanese soy sauce (shoyu)

3 x 2.5cm/1in cubes fresh ginger, the younger the better

10-12 shallots or small pickling onions, left whole

10-15 small garlic cloves, left whole

2 tbsp tamarind paste (page 7) or fresh lemon juice

2 tbsp dark muscovado sugar

salt (optional)

FOR THE CURRY PASTE

3-8 dried hot red chillies

2cm/¾in cube fresh galangal, coarsely chopped or 5 slices dried galangal, coarsely chopped or 2cm/¾in cube fresh ginger, coarsely chopped

2 sticks fresh lemon grass or 2 tbsp dried sliced lemon grass

100g/3½oz shallots or onions, coarsely chopped

10 large garlic cloves, chopped

1 tsp shrimp or anchovy paste

1 tbsp ground coriander seeds

2 tsp ground cumin seeds

½ tsp ground turmeric

1 Make the curry paste: place 250ml/9fl oz water in a bowl and crumble in the dried chillies, the more chillies you use the hotter the dish. If using dried galangal and dried lemon grass, add to the water as well. Leave to soak for 30 minutes. If using fresh lemon grass, cut into fine slices crossways, starting from the bottom and going up the stalk about 15cm/6in; discard the straw-like top.

2 Place the soaked chillies, galangal and lemon grass and the soaking liquid along with the remaining curry paste ingredients into a blender. If using fresh galangal or ginger or lemon grass, add now. Process until smooth.

3 In a bowl, combine the pork, curry paste and soy sauce and marinate for 30 minutes. Cut the ginger into very thin slices. Stack a few slices at a time together and cut into matchstick strips.

4 Place the pork and its marinade into a wide, heavy, non-stick frying pan and simmer gently for 15-20 minutes or until the meat starts to release its fat. Increase the heat and stir fry for about 10 minutes or until the spice mixture begins to dry out and brown. Add 450ml/16fl oz of water, the ginger strips, whole shallots and garlic cloves. Simmer, covered, for 45 minutes or until the meat is tender. Add the tamarind paste and brown sugar. Mix and taste, adding more of each if you need it, then add salt, if liked. Cook for 2–3 minutes to allow the flavours to develop and mingle.

Nutrition notes per serving: *391 calories, Protein 46g, Carbohydrate 17g, Fat 16g, Saturated fat 5g, Fibre 2g, Added sugar 8g, Salt 1.49g.*

⊛ *The curry paste and finished dish can each be frozen for 2 months. Simply defrost the paste and bring to room temperature before using. Defrost the curry, then reheat until piping hot.*

TIP

You can use boneless pork from the loin or shoulder. A little fat in the meat will keep it more tender. You can even cut the meat off chops, saving the bones to make stock to use later in soup.

PORK OR LAMB VINDALOO ✹

The essential ingredients for this Portuguese-inspired Indian dish are wine vinegar and garlic. The addition of mustard seeds, cumin, turmeric and chillies make it specifically colonial Goan. Vindaloos, which can also be made from beef, are very, very hot. Goans would use four teaspoons of chilli powder. Under my husband's 'spare-me' gaze I have used half a teaspoon to make a mild dish. It is up to you. You can cook this in a pressure cooker if you prefer. Most Vindaloo recipes involve grinding mustard seeds in vinegar. To save this step, I use grainy French Pommery mustard (Moutarde de Meaux) which already contains vinegar. It works beautifully.

Serves 3–4

1½ tbsp grainy French mustard

1½ tsp ground cumin

¾ tsp ground turmeric

½–1 tsp chilli powder

1 tsp salt

1 tsp red wine vinegar

3 tbsp vegetable oil

115g/4oz onions, cut into fine half-rings

6 large garlic cloves, crushed

550g boned hand of pork or shoulder of lamb, cut into 2.5cm/1in cubes

150ml/¼ pint canned coconut milk, well stirred

1 Combine the mustard, cumin, turmeric, chilli powder, salt and vinegar in a cup and mix well.

2 Heat the oil in a large, non-stick frying pan and when hot, add the onions and stir fry until golden. Add the garlic and stir fry for 30 seconds, then add the spice paste and stir fry for 1 minute.

3 Add the meat and stir fry for 3 minutes, then add the coconut milk and 150ml/¼ pint water if you are going to cook in a pressure cooker or 250ml/9fl oz if continuing to cook in the frying pan. (Transfer to a pressure cooker now, if using.) Cover and either bring up to pressure, or to the boil if you are using the frying pan. Reduce heat to a simmer and cook for 20 minutes in a pressure cooker and for 1 hour in the frying pan or until the pork is cooked completely through.

Nutrition notes per serving for three: *427 calories, Protein 41g, Carbohydrate 9g, Fat 26g, Saturated fat 6g, Fibre 1g, Added sugar none, Salt 2.47g.*

✹ *Cool quickly, then freeze. Can be frozen for up to 2 months. To serve, defrost in the fridge, then reheat until piping hot.*

TIP

Many recipes call for ground spices. In India, we generally buy our spices whole and then grind them ourselves when we need them. They have much more flavour this way. You probably already know the difference between freshly ground black pepper and ground pepper that has been sitting around for a month. The same applies to all spices. Use a clean coffee grinder and grind limited quantities so that the spices do not lose their flavour. Buying ground spices is perfectly all right as long as you know that they will be less potent as time goes on.

GOAN-STYLE HOT AND SOUR PORK ✵

The Hindus and Muslims of India do not, generally, eat pork but Indian Christians do. This dish, with its semi-Portuguese name suggesting that the meat is cooked with wine (or vinegar) and garlic, is a contribution from the Konkani-speaking Christians of western India. You can control the heat of this curry by putting in just as many red chillies as you think you can manage. Serve with mounds of fluffy rice.

Serves 6

2 tsp cumin seeds

2–3 dried hot red chillies

1 tsp black peppercorns

1 tsp cardamom seeds (See Tip)

7.5cm/3in cinnamon stick

1½ tsp black mustard seeds

1 tsp fenugreek seeds

5 tbsp white wine vinegar

1½–2 tsp salt

1 tsp light muscovado sugar

10 tbsp vegetable oil

175–200g/6–7oz onions, sliced into fine half-rings

900g boneless pork shoulder, trimmed and cut into 2.5cm/1in cubes

2.5cm/1in cube fresh root ginger, coarsely chopped

1 small whole head garlic, cloves separated

1 tbsp ground coriander

½ tsp ground turmeric

1   Grind the cumin seeds, red chillies, peppercorns, cardamom seeds, cinnamon, black mustard seeds and fenugreek seeds in a clean coffee grinder or spice grinder. Transfer to a bowl, add the vinegar, salt and sugar, mix and set aside.

2   Heat the oil in a wide, heavy pan and when hot, add the onions and fry, stirring frequently, until brown and crisp. Remove with a slotted spoon (reserve the oil) and place in a blender or food processor. Add two to three tablespoons of water and purée the onions. Add to the spices in the bowl. (This is the vindaloo paste.)

3   Pat the meat dry with kitchen paper. Place the ginger and garlic in a blender or food processor, add two to three tablespoons of water and blend to a smooth paste. Reheat the oil in the pan and when hot, add the pork cubes, a few at a time and brown lightly on all sides. Remove and keep warm. When all the pork is cooked, add the ginger-garlic paste to the pan. Reduce the heat, stir the paste for a few seconds, then add the coriander and turmeric and stir.

4   Return the meat and its juices to the pan, add the vindaloo paste and 250ml/9fl oz of water and bring to the boil. Cover and simmer gently for 1 hour or until the pork is tender, stirring occasionally.

Nutrition notes per serving: 429 calories, Protein 33g, Carbohydrate 7g, Fat 30g, Saturated fat 6g, Fibre 1g, Added sugar 1g, Salt 1.47g.

✵ The curry paste and finished dish can each be frozen for 2 months. Simply defrost the paste and bring to room temperature before using. Defrost the curry, then reheat until piping hot.

TIP

Cardamom, a highly aromatic spice, is generally sold in its pod form. If you cannot find cardamom seeds, break open the cardamom pods and scrape out the seeds. Indians like to use the green pods, but most supermarkets seem to stock the bleached, less aromatic whitish pods. If you are using cardamom pods whole, they should not be eaten. Just leave them on the side of your plate.

KASHMIRI RED LAMB STEW
(KASHMIRI ROGAN JOSH) ✳

Kashmiri Hindus do not eat any onions or garlic and they often use dry, powdered ginger instead of fresh. This is their version of rogan josh. Rogan josh gets its name from its rich, red appearance. The red appearance, in turn, is derived from ground red chillies which are used quite generously. If you want your dish to have the right colour and not be very hot, combine paprika with cayenne pepper in any proportion that you like. Just make sure that your paprika is fresh and has a good red colour. Serve with a green vegetable, plain long grain rice and a relish (pages 59–60).

Serves 4–6

1 tbsp fennel seeds

750ml/1¼ pints natural yogurt (See Tip)

3 tbsp vegetable oil

2cm/¾in cinnamon stick

½ tsp whole cloves

pinch of ground asafoetida (optional)

1.5kg stewing meat (with bone) from lamb shoulder and neck, cut into 5cm/2in cubes

2½ tsp salt or to taste

4 tsp bright red paprika mixed with ¼–1 tsp cayenne pepper

1½ tsp powdered ginger

¼ tsp Garam masala (page 62)

1 Grind the fennel seeds in a spice grinder or clean coffee grinder until fine. Place the yogurt in a bowl and beat with a fork or whisk until smooth and creamy.

2 Heat the oil in a large pan and when hot, add the cinnamon and cloves, then add the ground asafoetida, if using, the lamb and the salt. Stir and cook, still over a high heat, for 5 minutes. Add the paprika and cayenne and give the meat a good stir. Slowly add the yogurt (125–150ml/4fl oz–¼ pint at a time), stirring the meat vigorously as you do so. Keep cooking over a high heat until all the liquid has boiled away and the meat pieces have browned slightly.

3 Add the fennel and ginger and stir the meat, then add 850ml/1½ pints water, cover but leave the lid slightly ajar. Reduce the heat and cook for 30 minutes, then cover completely and cook over a low heat for 45 minutes or until the meat is tender, stirring occasionally. Make sure there is always some liquid in the pan.

4 Remove the lid and add the garam masala. You should have a thick reddish-brown sauce. If it is too thin, boil some of the liquid away.

Nutrition notes per serving for four: *743 calories, Protein 52g, Carbohydrate 16g, Fat 53g, Saturated fat 23g, Fibre none, Added sugar none, Salt 3.90g.*

✳ *Cool quickly, then freeze. Can be frozen for up to 1 month. To serve, defrost in the fridge, then reheat until piping hot.*

TIP

Yogurt adds a creamy texture and delicate tartness to sauces, but it curdles when it is heated. Always add a little at a time, stir and fry until it is absorbed and 'accepted' by the sauce, then add the next batch.

EASY BEEF CURRY
(KAENG PHET NUA) ✻

In this curry from Thailand, I use beef skirt which is such a tender cut of meat it requires hardly any cooking at all. I only stand at the cooker for 12 minutes. Eight minutes are spent frying the spices and the other four cooking the beef. This is perfect for a small dinner party.

Serves 4

450g beef skirt

125–140g/4½–5oz red pepper, seeded and coarsely chopped

115g/4oz onions, coarsely chopped

4 large garlic cloves, coarsely chopped

1 tsp shrimp or anchovy paste

½ tsp chilli powder

8 tbsp vegetable oil

2 tbsp fish sauce or 1 tbsp soy sauce mixed with 1 tbsp water and ¼ tsp sugar

250ml/9fl oz canned coconut milk, well stirred

½ tsp salt

4 fresh or dried kaffir lime leaves (See Tip)

10–15 fresh basil leaves, torn

10–15 fresh mint leaves, torn

1 Cut the beef against the grain into pieces 5–7.5cm/2–3in long, 2.5cm/1in wide and 2–3mm/¹⁄₁₆–⅛in thick. If you have bought the meat in a long, thin continuous piece, cut it into 7.5cm/3in segments, then cut each segment against the grain, holding the knife diagonally to your work surface. This will give the required width.

2 Combine the red pepper, onions, garlic, shrimp paste and chilli powder in a blender and process until smooth, adding a tablespoon or so of water only if you need to.

3 Heat the oil in a wide, shallow pan or frying pan and when hot, add the spice paste and stir fry for 7–8 minutes or until the paste turns dark and separates from the oil.

4 Add the meat and fish sauce, stir and cook for 2 minutes. Stir in the coconut milk, then add the salt and dried kaffir lime leaves, if using. If the kaffir lime leaves are fresh, tear in half and remove the centre vein before adding. Add the basil and mint, stir once, turn off the heat, then serve.

Nutrition notes per serving: 388 calories, Protein 25g, Carbohydrate 10g, Fat 28g, Saturated fat 5g, Fibre 1g, Added sugar 1g, Salt 1.80g.

✻ Cool quickly, then freeze. Can be frozen for up to 2 months. To serve, defrost in the fridge, then reheat until piping hot.

TIP

Kaffir lime leaves have a very distinctive appearance, like a figure of eight with two leaves joined together base to tip. Any leftover leaves can be stored in a plastic bag in the freezer. They are sometimes available dried at Far Eastern and some Chinese grocers. If you cannot find them use a 7.5x1cm/3x½in strip of lemon rind cut into fine julienne strips. Add to the curry at the same time as the mint and basil leaves.

Eggs & Poultry

EGG CURRY (GULAI TELOR) Ⓥ

This is one of my favourite egg curries. It is hot and spicy and quite typical of Malaysian food. Served with plain rice and salad, it is perfect for a Sunday lunch. I have been known to serve it with crusty bread or with thick toast. In Malaysia the spices are pounded very finely on stone. Since I can never quite manage to get the same effect in a blender, I strain the coarse particles out of the curry sauce before putting the eggs into it. Traditionally, this is made with 20–30 dried hot red chillies and it is hot and good. I tone it down by using 10–15 chillies and it is fairly hot but you can use as few as two chillies if you want it very mild. This can be made a day in advance, kept in the fridge, then reheated until piping hot.

Serves 6–8

2–15 dried hot red chillies, crumbled

½ tsp whole black peppercorns

2 tbsp whole coriander seeds

1 stick fresh lemon grass or
3 tbsp dried sliced lemon grass
or 1 tbsp grated lemon rind

4cm/1½in cube fresh galangal,
coarsely chopped or 8 large slices
dried galangal (optional)

4cm/1½in cube fresh ginger,
coarsely chopped

¾ tsp ground turmeric

18 eggs

9 tbsp vegetable oil

100g/3½oz shallots or onions,
finely sliced

5 garlic cloves, finely sliced

1 litre/1¾ pints coconut milk,
well stirred

3 tbsp tamarind paste (page 7)
or 2 tbsp fresh lime juice

2½ tsp salt

1 tsp sugar

280g/10oz tomatoes

4 fresh hot green chillies (See Tip,
page 40), 4 fresh hot red chillies
(See Tip) and fresh mint sprigs

1   Place the dried chillies, peppercorns, coriander seeds, dried lemon grass and dried galangal, if using, in a bowl and add 350ml/12fl oz of water. Leave to soak for at least 1 hour. If you are using fresh lemon grass, slice crossways very finely, start at the root end and go up about 15cm/6in; discard the straw-like top.

2   Place the soaked ingredients and the soaking liquid, the fresh lemon grass (if you are using lemon rind, add with the tomatoes at the end) and fresh galangal, if using, the ginger and turmeric in a blender and process thoroughly. Add another few tablespoons of water if needed to make a paste.

3   Place all the eggs in a large pan, cover well with water and bring to the boil. Reduce the heat to low and simmer for about 12 minutes until the eggs are hard-boiled. Shell under cold running water.

4   Heat the oil in a wide, non-stick pan and when hot, stir fry the shallots and garlic until golden. Pour in the paste from the blender and stir fry for 10 minutes or until the oil separates and the paste turns dark. Stir in the coconut milk, then add the tamarind paste, salt and sugar. Mix well and adjust seasoning.

5   Bring to a simmer, stirring, and as soon as the sauce begins to bubble, turn off the heat. Strain through a sieve, pushing through as much liquid as possible. Return the sauce to the pan and add the eggs. (This much of the dish can be prepared a day ahead and chilled.)

6   If the tomatoes are small, cut into wedges; if they are large, cut into 2.5cm/1in dice. Just before serving, bring the curry to a simmer, add the tomatoes and stir a few times, then transfer to a serving bowl and top with the chillies and mint.

Nutrition notes per serving for six: *442 calories, Protein 21g, Carbohydrate 13g, Fat 34g, Saturated fat 6g, Fibre 1g, Added sugar none, Salt 1.84g.*

TIP

The fresh chillies give the dish a Malaysian look. If fresh red chillies are unavailable, simply use twice as many green ones. You can even use slivers cut from fresh red and green peppers, if you prefer.

HEARTY CHICKEN CURRY WITH POTATOES
(LAUK AYAM) ✸

Malaysian curries are among the best in East Asia and this one from Kuala Lumpur is extra spicy and rich and better than most. It can be served with almost any bread, from crusty French and Italian loaves to pitta breads and Indian chapattis. It can also be served with rice. This curry seems to improve with time, so can easily be made a day in advance and kept in the fridge. Use less than the recommended quantity of chilli powder if you prefer a mild curry.

Serves 6

6–8 cardamom pods

6 whole cloves

2 whole star anise

2 x 5cm/2in cinnamon sticks

2 tbsp whole fennel seeds

1½ tbsp whole cumin seeds

4 tbsp ground coriander seeds

1½–2 tsp chilli powder or to taste

1 tbsp paprika

4 x 2.5cm/1in cubes fresh ginger, coarsely chopped

3 large garlic cloves, coarsely chopped

4 medium onions, 3 coarsely chopped and 1 finely sliced

1.8kg skinless chicken pieces, preferably legs

175ml/6fl oz vegetable oil

450g/1lb potatoes, cut into 2.5cm/1in cubes and left in water

1 tbsp salt

200ml/7fl oz canned coconut milk, well stirred

good handful fresh mint leaves, coarsely chopped

1 Place the cardamom pods, cloves, star anise, cinnamon, fennel and cumin in a clean coffee grinder or spice grinder, then grind as finely as possible. Transfer to a bowl. Add the ground coriander, chilli powder, paprika, eight tablespoons of water and mix to a thick paste.

2 Place the ginger, garlic, the three chopped onions and four tablespoons of water in a blender and process to a smooth paste.

3 Cut the chicken legs into thighs and drumsticks. If using breasts, cut in half. Heat the oil in a large, wide pan and when hot, add the sliced onion and stir fry until golden brown. Stir in the paste from the blender and the spice paste from the bowl. Stir fry for 10–12 minutes or until the mixture is well fried and dark.

4 Add 700ml/1¼ pints water, the chicken, drained potatoes and salt and bring to a simmer. Cover, lower the heat and cook gently for 30 minutes or until the chicken is tender. Stir in the coconut milk and cook for a further minute, then add the mint leaves. The oil floating on the top of the curry may be removed before serving.

Nutrition notes per serving: *519 calories, Protein 31g, Carbohydrate 28g, Fat 32g, Saturated fat 5g, Fibre 2g, Added sugar none, Salt 2.94g.*

✸ *Cool quickly, then freeze. Can be frozen for up to 2 months. To serve, defrost in the fridge, then reheat until piping hot.*

TIP

Fresh ginger should be peeled before it can be chopped, sliced, grated, or made into a paste. If a recipe requires 2.5cm/1in of ginger to be grated, you will find that it is easier to grate that length while it is still attached to the large knob. When buying, look for pieces that are not too wrinkled but have a taut skin. Ginger should be stored in a cool, dry, airy basket along with your garlic, onions and potatoes. If you use it infrequently, 'store' ginger by planting it in a dry, sandy soil. Water occasionally. Your ginger will not only survive, but will also sprout fresh knobs. Whenever you need some, dig it up, break off a knob, then replant.

QUICK CHICKEN KORMA
(MURGH KORMA) ✺

When trying to cook fast, it helps to have all the right tools and utensils at hand. Here, a blender to make the ginger-garlic paste and a frying pan or sauté pan wide enough to hold all the chicken in a single layer will be of great help. This dish can be made a day in advance and kept in the fridge. It reheats well. In India, we almost always remove the skin of chicken before cooking. The flavour of the spices penetrates the chicken much better and the entire dish is less fatty. It is very easy to remove the skin, just hold an edge with kitchen paper so that it does not slip, and pull.

Serves 4

4cm/1½in piece fresh root ginger, coarsely chopped

5–6 garlic cloves, coarsely chopped

6 tbsp vegetable oil

3 bay leaves

5cm/2in cinnamon stick

8 cardamom pods

4 whole cloves

¼ tsp black or ordinary cumin seeds

125g/4½oz onions, finely chopped

1 tbsp ground coriander

1 tbsp ground cumin

3 canned plum tomatoes, chopped

1.5kg skinless chicken pieces, cut into serving portions

¼–1 tsp chilli powder

¾ tsp salt

3 tbsp single cream

1 Place the ginger, garlic and three tablespoons of water in a blender and process to a smooth paste.

2 Heat the oil in a wide frying pan and when very hot, add the bay leaves, cinnamon, cardamom pods, cloves and cumin seeds. Stir once or twice, then add the onions. Stir fry for 3 minutes or until the onions turn brownish, then add the paste, ground coriander and cumin and fry for 1 minute.

3 Add the tomatoes, fry for 1 minute, then add the chicken, chilli powder, salt and 250ml/9fl oz of water. Bring to the boil, cover and reduce the heat and cook for 15 minutes, turning the chicken pieces occasionally.

4 Add the cream and cook, uncovered, over a high heat, stirring gently, for 7–8 minutes or until the sauce has thickened.

Nutrition notes per serving: *423 calories, Protein 37g, Carbohydrate 8g, Fat 28g, Saturated fat 6g, Fibre 1g, Added sugar none, Salt 1.39g.*

✺ *Cool quickly, then freeze. Can be frozen for up to 2 months. To serve, defrost in the fridge, then reheat until piping hot.*

TIP

Cloves are the dried flower buds of a tropical evergreen tree that grows best near the sea. The main clove growing area is now the island of Zanzibar. They contain a powerful and aromatic essential oil with antiseptic and anaesthetic qualities often used to relieve toothache. Indians suck on cloves as a mouth freshener.

Fish & Shellfish

CURRIED TUNA (TUNA KI KARI)

Eat this in sandwiches, on toast and with salads. Do not drain the oil from the tuna.

Serves 2–3

1½ tbsp vegetable oil

55g/2oz onions, cut into fine half-rings

1 garlic clove, very finely chopped

1 tsp curry powder

180g can tuna in oil

½–1 fresh green chilli, finely sliced

1cm/½in fresh root ginger, sliced

2–3 tbsp chopped fresh coriander

salt and freshly ground black pepper

1   Heat the oil in a non-stick frying pan and when hot, add the onions and garlic. Stir fry until the onions turn brown at the edges, then add the curry powder and stir.

2   Stir in the tuna, breaking up any large lumps, then reduce the heat and add the chilli, ginger and coriander. Stir to mix, check seasoning and add salt if needed. Add a generous amount of black pepper, mix well and turn off the heat. Serve hot, at room temperature or cold.

Nutrition notes per serving for two: *336 calories, Protein 23g, Carbohydrate 4g, Fat 26g, Saturated fat 4g, Fibre 1g, Added sugar none, Salt 1.12g.*

SPICY PRAWN AND CUCUMBER CURRY (GULAI LABU)

This Malaysian curry is actually made with bottle gaud – a pale green vegetable shaped like a bowling pin. You can easily use cucumber instead as its taste is similar when cooked.

Serves 4–6

350g/12oz raw prawns, peeled and deveined

115g/4oz shallots or onions

6 garlic cloves

2 tbsp ground coriander seeds

1 tbsp ground fennel seeds (See Tip)

1 tsp ground white pepper or to taste

1 tbsp ground cumin seeds

1 tsp ground turmeric

3–4 dried hot red chillies

280g/10oz cucumber, peeled and cut crossways into 1cm/½in rounds

¾–1 tsp salt

1 tsp sugar

400ml/14fl oz canned coconut milk

4 tbsp vegetable oil

1 tsp whole fennel seeds

1   Wash the prawns and pat dry. Very finely chop 85g/3oz of the shallots, then finely slice the remainder. Very finely chop four of the garlic cloves and cut the other two into fine slivers. Combine sliced shallots and slivered garlic; set aside.

2   In a medium pan, combine the chopped shallots, garlic, coriander, ground fennel seeds, white pepper, cumin, turmeric and 450ml/16fl oz of water. Crumble in the red chillies, stir and bring to the boil, then cook, uncovered, over a high heat, for 5 minutes.

3   Add the cucumber rounds and return to a simmer, cover and cook for 5 minutes. Add the prawns, salt and sugar and simmer gently for 1 minute, stirring. Stir in the coconut milk, bring the mixture to the boil, then reduce the heat and simmer for 1 minute, stirring occasionally.

4   Heat the oil and when hot, add the reserved shallots and garlic. Stir fry until golden, then add fennel seeds. Stir once and pour into pan containing the curry.

Nutrition notes per serving for four: *277 calories, Protein 20g, Carbohydrate 16g, Fat 15g, Saturated fat 1g, Fibre 1g, Added sugar 1g, Salt 1.72g.*

TIP

If you cannot buy ground fennel seeds, simply grind whole seeds in a clean coffee grinder, in a spice grinder or with a pestle and mortar.

FISH FILLETS IN CURRY SAUCE
('CURRY' DAR MACCHI)

Bland white sauces were anathema to the Indian cooks in Anglo-Indian households so they invariably added a few local seasonings to perk them up. Here is one such dish. You can use any fish fillets – cod, haddock or halibut. Fillets of dark, oily fish such as blue fish and mackerel are ideal. Buy thick fillets if possible, and if they are skinless, so much the better.

Serves 4–5

900g/2lb thick fish fillet or fillets (See Tip)

500ml/18fl oz milk

1 tsp salt

freshly ground black pepper

½ tsp chilli powder

¼ tsp ground turmeric

5 tbsp dried breadcrumbs, made from dried bread (See Tip) or shop-bought

55g/2oz unsalted butter

4 tbsp good curry powder

2 tbsp plain flour

3 tbsp finely chopped fresh coriander (See Tip, page 39)

2–3 tsp fresh lemon juice

1   Arrange a shelf in the upper third of the oven and preheat to its highest temperature. Place the fish in a deep dish. Combine the milk, salt, pepper, chilli powder and turmeric in a jug and pour over the fish. Leave to stand for 15 minutes.

2   Remove the fish with a slotted spoon (reserve the milk) and dust both sides with the breadcrumbs, pressing them so they stick. Place the fish in a shallow baking tray lined with foil, dot with half the butter and bake for 15 minutes.

3   Meanwhile, heat the milk and melt the remaining butter in a small, heavy pan. When the butter is bubbling, add the curry powder and stir for 1 minute. Add the flour and stir for 2 minutes. (It should keep bubbling.) Remove the pan from the heat and, using a whisk, beat in the hot milk. Return the pan to the heat and stir with the whisk until the sauce comes to the boil. Boil for 1 minute, whisking continuously, then add the coriander and lemon juice and stir to mix.

4   Place the fish on serving plates, pour over the sauce and serve. Any extra sauce can be served separately.

Nutrition notes per serving for four: *496 calories, Protein 48g, Carbohydrate 33g, Fat 20g, Saturated fat 11g, Fibre 4g, Added sugar none, Salt 2.23g.*

TIP

To make dried breadcrumbs: first make fresh white breadcrumbs. Stand a coarse grater in a large bowl. Rub bread chunks, crusts removed, on the grater to reduce to breadcrumbs. Alternatively, whizz bread chunks in a food processor. For dried crumbs: bake in a very low oven (or residual heat from cooking) without browning. Reduce to fine crumbs by whizzing in a processor.

STIR-FRIED PRAWNS IN AN AROMATIC TOMATO-CREAM SAUCE (BHAGARI JHINGA)

One of the aromas that I find very refreshing in this particular dish is that of fresh curry leaves. I know fresh curry leaves are not easy to find, but if you do come across them, buy extra and freeze flat in polythene bags. To take fresh curry leaves off the stem, just pull along the stem with your thumb and first finger and they will come right off. If you manage to find dried curry leaves, add to the cream sauce instead of frying with the prawns. If you cannot find fresh or dried curry leaves just do without. The dish will still taste superb. The actual cooking of this dish takes just minutes. The sauce can be made several hours in advance and kept in the fridge. The prawns could be peeled, deveined, washed, patted dry and left covered in the fridge overnight, if necessary. It is best served with rice.

Serves 4–5

FOR THE SAUCE

1 tbsp tomato purée

¾ tsp salt

¼ tsp sugar

1 tsp shop-bought garam masala

½ tsp ground roasted cumin seeds (See Tip)

pinch of chilli powder or to taste

3 tbsp finely chopped fresh coriander (See Tip, page 39)

1 fresh hot green chilli, finely chopped (See Tip, page 40)

1 tbsp fresh lemon juice

200ml/7fl oz canned coconut milk, well stirred or single cream

FOR THE PRAWNS

550g/1¼lb raw prawns, peeled and deveined

3 tbsp vegetable oil

1 tsp black mustard seeds

3 garlic cloves, finely chopped

10–15 fresh curry leaves

1 Make the sauce: combine the tomato purée, salt, sugar, garam masala, cumin seeds, chilli powder, coriander, chilli, lemon juice and one tablespoon of water in a bowl. Mix well, slowly add the coconut milk, mixing as you go, then set aside.

2 Wash the prawns and pat dry with kitchen paper. Heat the oil in a wok or frying pan and when hot, add the mustard seeds. As soon as they begin to pop – this takes just a few seconds – add the garlic and curry leaves. Stir until the garlic turns brown, then add the prawns. Stir fry until the prawns turn opaque most of the way through, then pour in the sauce. Reduce the heat and heat the sauce until it just begins to simmer, then serve. (The prawns should now be completely opaque.)

Nutrition notes per serving for four: *221 calories, Protein 26g, Carbohydrate 7g, Fat 10g, Saturated fat 1g, Fibre 1g, Added sugar 1g, Salt 1.81g.*

TIP

To make ground roasted cumin seeds: place four to five tablespoons of whole seeds in a small cast-iron frying pan over a medium heat. Stir the seeds and dry roast until they turn a few shades darker and emit a wonderful roasted aroma. Cool slightly, then grind in a clean coffee grinder or spice grinder. Store in a tightly closed jar. This is a useful spice to have on hand. It will last a good month or two though its flavour will gradually lessen.

SQUID OR SCALLOPS IN A SPINACH-TOMATO CURRY SAUCE
(SAMUNDAR KI KARI)

If you are in a hurry, it is best to buy cleaned squid. Scallops, of course, are sold ready for cooking. This dish can be served with rice or, oddly enough, noodles. It is superb for entertaining. If you prefer, substitute raw peeled prawns.

Serves 4

½ tsp chilli powder

½ tsp ground turmeric

1 tsp ground cumin

1 tsp ground coriander

1 tsp salt

freshly ground black pepper

1 tsp grainy French mustard

3 tbsp vegetable oil

1 tsp black or yellow mustard seeds

3–4 garlic cloves, finely chopped

1cm/½in piece fresh root ginger, finely chopped

150ml/¼ pint canned chopped tomatoes

115g/4oz fresh spinach, cut crossways into fine strips

550g/1¼lb cleaned sliced squid or whole scallops (See Tip)

125ml/4fl oz canned coconut milk, well stirred or single cream

1. Combine the chilli powder, turmeric, cumin, coriander, salt, black pepper, the mustard and two tablespoons of water in a bowl and set aside.

2. Heat the oil in a large, non-stick frying pan and when hot, put in the whole mustard seeds. As soon as they begin to pop – this takes just a few seconds – add the garlic and ginger. Stir fry until the garlic turns light brown, then add the spice paste and stir fry for 15 seconds.

3. Add the tomatoes and spinach, stir and cook for 1 minute, then add 250ml/ 9fl oz water and bring to a simmer. Simmer, uncovered, for 10 minutes, then add the squid or scallops. Increase the heat to high, stir and cook until the squid or scallops turn opaque. (This will happen quite fast.) Stir in the coconut milk, return to a simmer and cook for 30 seconds.

Nutrition notes per serving: *217 calories, Protein 24g, Carbohydrate 7g, Fat 11g, Saturated fat 1g, Fibre 1g, Added sugar none, Salt 2.43g.*

TIP

To prepare squid: twist the head (with the tentacles) off. Cut off the hard area near the eyes but retain the head. Squeeze or pull out all the soft matter inside the tubular body as well as the hard cartilage-like 'pen'. Peel the fine skin off the tubular body. Now wash both the body and head. Rub with one to two tablespoons of coarse salt, wash, rub again with salt, wash well, drain and pat dry. Cut the tubular body into 5mm/¼in rings. The head area and tentacles can be left whole or halved. You can buy fresh or frozen scallops loose (that is not freshly removed from their shells in front of you). Scallops that have been frozen are pure white and look milky, plump and moist. Fresh scallops are more translucent and creamy-grey rather than white.

Vegetable Dishes

CAULIFLOWER WITH GINGER, GARLIC AND GREEN CHILLIES
(SOOKHI GOBI) Ⓥ

The special taste comes from allowing the florets to brown slightly. Do not cut florets too small.

Serves 3–4

3 tbsp vegetable oil

½ tsp cumin seeds

½ tsp yellow mustard seeds

3 garlic cloves, finely chopped

2.5cm/1in fresh root ginger, sliced

450g/1lb cauliflower florets

1–3 fresh hot green chillies, sliced

¾ tsp salt

freshly ground black pepper

½ tsp shop–bought garam masala

pinch of chilli powder or to taste

1 Heat the oil in a wok over a high heat and when hot, add the cumin and mustard seeds. As soon as the mustard seeds begin to pop – this takes just a few seconds – add the garlic, ginger, cauliflower and chillies all at the same time. Stir fry for 5–7 minutes or until the cauliflower has turned slightly brown.

2 Add the salt, pepper and garam masala and chilli powder and give the florets a good toss. Stir in four tablespoons of water, cover and cook for 2 minutes.

Nutrition notes per serving for three: *168 calories, Protein 6g, Carbohydrate 7g, Fat 13g, Saturated fat 1g, Fibre 3g, Added sugar none, Salt 1.37g.*

CABBAGE STIR FRIED WITH RED PEPPER PASTE
(SALA LOBAK)

I discovered this dish in the remote hills of Western Sumatra in Indonesia.

Serves 4

115g/4oz red pepper, seeded and coarsely chopped

55g/2oz shallots or onions, chopped

2 large garlic cloves, chopped

½ tsp shrimp or anchovy paste (optional)

¼ tsp chilli powder

6 tbsp vegetable oil

450g/1lb dark outer cabbage leaves or spring greens, shredded (See Tip)

½ tsp salt

1 Combine the red pepper, shallots, garlic, shrimp paste, if using, chilli powder and three tablespoons of water in a blender and process to a coarse paste.

2 Heat a wok over a high heat, then add the oil and the spice paste. Stir fry for 5 minutes or until the oil separates and the mixture has a dark red appearance. Add the cabbage and salt and stir fry for 30 seconds.

3 Cover tightly, reduce the heat and cook for 8–10 minutes or until the cabbage is cooked. (No water should be needed, but check after 5–6 minutes.)

Nutrition notes per serving: *202 calories, Protein 4g, Carbohydrate 6g, Fat 18g, Saturated fat 2g, Fibre 5g, Added sugar none, Salt 0.70g.*

TIP

Use some of the inner cabbage if you are slightly short of dark leaves.

MUSHROOM CURRY
(SHORVEDAR KHUMBI) Ⓥ

Most of the fresh mushrooms sold in supermarkets are cultivated varieties of the field mushroom and are picked at varying stages of maturity. Button mushrooms are closed, small, white and picked very young. Cup mushrooms are partly open and are available as closed cup (with the skin still closed beneath the cap) or grown longer until the pink gills are exposed. Flat mushrooms are open with dark brown gills and because the flavour of mushrooms improves with age these are the most tasty. Chestnut mushrooms are dark beige-brown, about the same size as cup mushrooms, but have more flavour than their white cousins. Fresh oyster and shiitake mushrooms, now becoming more available, are used mainly in Oriental cooking. I have used ordinary white mushrooms but you can make this with almost any seasonal variety. Whichever type you choose cut into large, chunky pieces so they do not get lost in the sauce.

Serves 4

4cm/1½in piece fresh root ginger, chopped

115g/4oz onions, chopped

3 garlic cloves, chopped

6 tbsp vegetable oil

450g/1lb large mushrooms, halved or quartered

3 tbsp natural yogurt

1 tsp tomato purée

2 tsp ground coriander

¾ tsp salt

⅛–¼ tsp chilli powder

2 tbsp chopped fresh coriander (See Tip)

1   Place the ginger, onions, garlic and three tablespoons of water in a blender and process until smooth. Heat half the oil in a non-stick frying pan and when hot, add the mushrooms. Stir fry for 2–3 minutes or until the mushrooms have lost their raw look. Transfer pan contents to a bowl and wipe the pan.

2   Add the remaining oil to the pan and when hot, add the spice paste and stir fry for 3–4 minutes until it starts turning brown. Add one tablespoon of yogurt and fry for 30 seconds, then repeat twice more. Add the tomato purée and fry for 30 seconds, then add the ground coriander and stir.

3   Stir in 300ml/½ pint water, the mushrooms and their juices, the salt and chilli powder and stir. Simmer for 5 minutes, then sprinkle over the fresh coriander and serve.

Nutrition notes per serving: *194 calories, Protein 4g, Carbohydrate 6g, Fat 17g, Saturated fat 2g, Fibre 2g, Added sugar none, Salt 1.06g.*

TIP

Coriander is one of India's favourite herbs. It grows to 15–20cm/6–8in and is used just as parsley might be, both as a garnish and for its flavour. Just the top, leafy section is used, although the stems are sometimes thrown into pulse dishes for their aroma. To store fresh coriander, put in its unwashed state, roots and all, into a container filled with water. Pull a polythene bag over the coriander and the container and keep in the fridge. It should last for weeks. Every other day pick off and discard yellowing leaves. If you cannot find fresh coriander, use parsley as a substitute.

NEW POTATOES WITH CUMIN (ZEERA ALOO) ⓥ

This is one of my favourite ways of preparing new potatoes, Indian-style. You can serve them with an Indian meal or, if you like, Western dishes.

Serves 4–6

900g/2lb new potatoes

1 tbsp salt, plus ¾ tsp

2½ tbsp vegetable oil

1 tsp cumin seeds

1 tsp ground cumin

½ tsp shop-bought garam masala

⅛–¼ tsp chilli powder

2–3 tbsp chopped fresh coriander (See Tip, page 39)

1 Scrub the potatoes and place in a pan. Cover with water to come about 2.5cm/1in above them, add one tablespoon of salt and bring to the boil. Cover and cook the potatoes until just tender, then drain.

2 Heat the oil in a large frying pan and when hot, add the cumin seeds. Let the seeds sizzle for a few seconds, then add the potatoes. Reduce the heat and brown the potatoes lightly on all sides.

3 Reduce the heat to low and add remaining salt, the ground cumin, garam masala and chilli powder. Cook, stirring, for 1 minute. Add the fresh coriander just before serving and toss to mix.

Nutrition notes per serving for four: *232 calories, Protein 5g, Carbohydrate 38g, Fat 8g, Saturated fat 1g, Fibre 2g, Added sugar none, Salt 1.32g.*

GREEN PEAS IN A CREAMY SAUCE (MATAR MAKHANI) ⓥ

In this recipe frozen peas can be used to great advantage. The cream sauce can be made a day in advance and kept in the fridge. This dish can be served with all Indian meals and it also goes well with lamb and pork roasts.

Serves 5–6

¼ tsp sugar

½ tsp ground cumin

½ tsp Garam masala (page 62)

¾ tsp salt

¼–½ tsp chilli powder

1 tbsp tomato purée

175ml/6fl oz single cream

1 tbsp fresh lemon juice

2 tbsp chopped fresh coriander

1 fresh hot green chilli, finely chopped (See Tip)

3 tbsp vegetable oil

½ tsp cumin seeds

½ tsp black or yellow mustard seeds

2 x 285g packets frozen peas, thawed under warm water and drained

1 Combine the sugar, cumin, garam masala, salt, chilli powder and tomato purée, then slowly add two tablespoons of water, mixing as you go. Slowly stir in the cream, add the lemon juice, coriander and green chilli. Mix and set aside.

2 Heat the oil in a large frying pan and when hot, add the cumin and mustard seeds. As soon as the mustard seeds begin to pop – this takes just a few seconds – add the peas and stir fry for 30 seconds. Add the cream sauce and cook, over a high heat, for 1½–2 minutes or until the sauce has thickened, stirring gently.

Nutrition notes per serving for five: *217 calories, Protein 8g, Carbohydrate 14g, Fat 15g, Saturated fat 5g, Fibre 6g, Added sugar 1g, Salt 0.87g.*

TIP

Be careful when handling cut green chillies. Refrain from touching your eyes or mouth; wash your hands as soon as possible, otherwise you will 'burn' your skin with the irritant the chillies contain. If you want the green chilli flavour without most of the heat, remove the white seeds.

SWEET AND SOUR OKRA
(KUTCHHI BHINDI) Ⓥ

This dish is an absolutely wonderful way to cook okra, also known as ladies' fingers or bhindi. It tastes best when made with young, tender pods. Okra are from 4–13cm/1½–5in long and both pods and seeds are eaten. Inside the pods is a sticky juice which gives a rich, silky finish to dishes. Okra are most readily available here from December through to July, although they can be found in specialist shops at other times of the year. When buying choose okra without any brown marks, which indicates they are past their best, and ones that snap easily with no bend. Trim pods by cutting off the two ends. The top end is usually trimmed with a paring knife to leave a cone-shaped head while only a tiny piece of the bottom is cut off. If the ridges are tough or damaged, scrape them carefully with a sharp knife.

Serves 4–6

7 medium garlic cloves

1 dried hot red chilli (use half if you want a very mild dish)

2 tsp ground cumin

1 tsp ground coriander

½ tsp ground turmeric (See Tip)

4 tbsp vegetable oil

1 tsp cumin seeds

400g/14oz fresh tender okra, cut into 2cm/¾in lengths

1 tsp salt

1 tsp sugar

about 4 tsp fresh lemon juice

1   Place the garlic and chilli in a blender with three tablespoons of water and blend until smooth. Transfer to bowl, add the ground cumin, coriander and turmeric, mix well and set aside.

2   Heat the oil in a 23cm/9in frying pan and when hot, add the cumin seeds. As soon as they begin to sizzle – this takes just a few seconds – reduce the heat and pour in the spice mixture. Stir fry for 1 minute, then stir in the okra, salt, sugar, lemon juice and four tablespoons of water.

3   Bring to a gentle simmer, cover tightly and cook over a low heat for 10 minutes or until the okra is tender. If you need to cook for longer you may need to add a little more water.

Nutrition notes per serving for four: *162 calories, Protein 4g, Carbohydrate 8g, Fat 13g, Saturated fat 1g, Fibre 4g, Added sugar 1g, Salt 1.28g.*

TIP

Turmeric is the spice that makes many Indian foods yellow. Apart from its mild, earthy flavour, it is used mainly because it is a digestive and antiseptic. Fresh turmeric is not unlike ginger but smaller in size and more delicate in appearance. Use fresh if you can. A 2.5cm/1in piece is equal to about half a teaspoon of ground. Like ginger, it needs to be peeled and ground which is best done with a little water in a blender. Use turmeric carefully as it can stain.

SPINACH WITH GINGER AND GREEN CHILLIES

(SAAG BHAJI) Ⓥ

Indians tend to eat a lot of greens, sometimes a single variety on its own, sometimes mixed with other greens.

Serves 4

2cm/¾in piece fresh root ginger

3 tbsp vegetable oil

500g/18oz fresh spinach (See Tip)

2–3 fresh hot green chillies, chopped (See Tip, page 40)

½ tsp salt

½ tsp shop-bought garam masala

¼ tsp sugar

pinch of chilli powder

1   Cut the ginger crossways, into very thin slices. Stack a few slices together at a time and cut into very fine slivers.

2   Heat the oil in a wok or large, wide pan over a high heat and when very hot, add the ginger and stir until it starts to brown. Add the spinach and chillies and cook until the spinach has wilted. Add the salt, garam masala, sugar and chilli powder. Stir and cook for 5 minutes, then serve.

Nutrition notes per serving: *111 calories, Protein 4g, Carbohydrate 3g, Fat 9g, Saturated fat 1g, Fibre 3g, Added sugar 1g, Salt 1.07g.*

TIP

I like to keep the spinach leaves whole, but if they are very large you might need to chop them coarsely.

GENTLY STEWED BEETROOTS (TARIDAR CHUKANDAR) Ⓥ

Any beetroots can be used for this stew-like dish. My own favourite is *chioggia*, a very early Italian variety. It is small, sweet with radish-red skin and striated red and pale yellow flesh.

Serves 4–6

3 tbsp vegetable oil

1 tsp cumin seeds

1 bay leaf

250ml/9fl oz canned chopped tomatoes

1 tsp ground cumin

1 tsp ground coriander

¼ tsp ground turmeric

¼ tsp chilli powder

900g/2lb raw beetroots, peeled and cut into 2.5cm/1in chunks

¾ tsp salt

1   Heat the oil in a wide, medium pan over a high heat and when hot, add the cumin seeds and bay leaf. As soon as the bay leaf darkens slightly – this just takes a few seconds – add the tomatoes, ground cumin, coriander, turmeric, chilli powder, beetroots, salt and 350ml/12fl oz water.

2   Stir and bring to the boil, cover and simmer for 30–40 minutes or until the beetroots are tender.

Nutrition notes per serving for four: *200 calories, Protein 6g, Carbohydrate 25g, Fat 9g, Saturated fat 1g, Fibre 5g, Added sugar none, Salt 1.70g.*

Pulses

SMALL YELLOW SPLIT PEAS (CHANA DAL) ⓥ

Of all the dals (split peas), this one perhaps has the 'meatiest' taste. At its best, it also has a gentle sweetness. If you cannot find chana dal substitute yellow split peas.

Serves 4–6

225g/8oz chana dal or yellow split peas, washed and drained

½ tsp ground turmeric

2 thin slices unpeeled fresh root ginger

¾–1 tsp salt

¼ tsp Garam masala (page 62)

3 tbsp Ghee (page 62) or vegetable oil

½ tsp cumin seeds

1–2 garlic cloves, chopped

¼–½ tsp red chilli powder

1 Place the dal in a heavy pan with 1.2 litres/2 pints water. Bring to the boil and remove any surface scum. Add the turmeric and ginger. Cover, leaving the lid slightly ajar (See Tip), reduce the heat and simmer gently for 1½ hours or until the dal is tender. Stir every 5 minutes or so during the last 30 minutes to prevent sticking. Add the salt and garam masala and stir to mix.

2 Heat the ghee in small frying pan and when hot, add the cumin seeds. A couple of seconds later, add the garlic and stir fry until the garlic pieces are lightly browned. Add the chilli powder to the pan, then remove from the heat and pour the entire contents into the dal pan. Stir to mix and serve.

Nutrition notes per serving for four: *264 calories, Protein 13g, Carbohydrate 29g, Fat 12g, Saturated fat 1g, Fibre trace, Added sugar none, Salt 1.05g.*

TIP

When cooking split peas, leave the lid of the pan slightly ajar to prevent the contents spilling over. They create a lot of thick froth as they cook and this blocks up the normal escape routes for the steam with the result that the pot boils over.

RED LENTILS 'TARKA' (MASOOR DAL) ⓥ

Indians tend to eat protein-rich legumes with many everyday meals. Often, these are prepared with just a flavouring, or 'tarka' (page 62).

Serves 6–8

350g/12oz red lentils, washed and drained

½ tsp ground turmeric

1¼–1½ tsp salt

3 tbsp Ghee (page 62) or vegetable oil

generous pinch of ground asafoetida

1 tsp cumin seeds

3–5 dried hot red chillies

1 Place the lentils in a heavy pan with 1.2 litres/2 pints of water and the turmeric. Stir and bring to a simmer. Leave the lid slightly ajar (See Tip). Cook over a low heat for 35–40 minutes, stirring occasionally, or until the lentils are tender. Add the salt, mix and leave covered over a low heat.

2 Heat the ghee in a frying pan over a fairly high heat and when hot, add the asafoetida followed by the cumin seeds. Let the cumin seeds sizzle for a few seconds, then add the chillies. As soon as they turn dark red – this takes just a few seconds – lift up the lid of the lentil pan and pour in the frying pan contents.

Nutrition notes per serving: *242 calories, Protein 14g, Carbohydrate 34g, Fat 7g, Saturated fat 1g, Fibre 3g, Added sugar none, Salt 0.28g.*

BLACK-EYED BEANS WITH MUSHROOMS
(LOBHIA AUR KHUMBI) ⓥ

Pulses – dried beans, split peas, and lentils – are a staple in India and help provide a large measure of the daily protein for families who eat meat rarely or are vegetarian. But pulses, by themselves, are an incomplete food and need to be complemented – at the same meal – with a grain (rice or bread) and a dairy product (such as yogurt or cheese). Black-eyed beans, greyish or beige ovals, graced with a large dot, are sold widely in all supermarkets and have a slightly smokey flavour. I like this bean dish so much I often find myself eating it with a spoon, all by itself. I serve it with Kashmiri red lamb stew (page 19). Rice or Indian breads should be served on the side.

Serves 6

225g/8oz dried black-eyed beans, picked over, washed and drained

6 tbsp vegetable oil

1 tsp cumin seeds

2.5cm/1in cinnamon stick

140g/5oz onions, chopped

4 garlic cloves, very finely chopped

225g/8oz mushrooms, cut through their stems into 3mm/⅛in thick slices

400g/14oz tomatoes, peeled and chopped (See Tip)

2 tsp ground coriander

1 tsp ground cumin

½ tsp ground turmeric

¼ tsp cayenne pepper

2 tsp salt

freshly ground black pepper

3 tbsp chopped fresh coriander (See Tip, page 39)

1 Place the beans in a heavy pan with 1.2 litres/2 pints water and bring to the boil. Cover, reduce the heat to low and simmer gently for 2 minutes. Turn off the heat and let the pan sit, covered and undisturbed, for 1 hour.

2 Heat the oil in a frying pan and when hot, add the cumin seeds and cinnamon stick. Let them sizzle for 5–6 seconds, then add the onions and garlic. Stir fry until the onions turn brown at the edges, then add the mushrooms and stir fry until wilted.

3 Stir in the tomatoes, coriander, cumin, turmeric and cayenne and cook for 1 minute. Cover, reduce the heat and let the mixture cook in its own juices for 10 minutes, then turn off the heat.

4 Bring the beans back to the boil, cover, reduce heat to low and simmer for 20–30 minutes or until the beans are tender. Add the mushroom mixture to the beans with the salt, black pepper and fresh coriander. Stir to mix and simmer, uncovered, for 30 minutes, stirring occasionally. Remove the cinnamon stick before serving.

Nutrition notes per serving: *247 calories, Protein 10g, Carbohydrate 25g, Fat 12g, Saturated fat 1g, Fibre 8g, Added sugar none, Salt 1.72g.*

TIP

To peel tomatoes: bring a pan of water to a rolling boil. Drop in the tomatoes for 15 seconds. Drain, rinse under cold water and peel. Now chop, making sure that you save all the juices that come out of them. In India, we very rarely seed tomatoes. Many people do not even bother to peel them, although I do feel that this improves the texture of the sauce.

CHICK PEAS COOKED IN TEA
(DHABAY KAY CHANAY) Ⓥ

The tea – leftover tea can be used – leaves no aftertaste. It just alters the colour of the chick peas. This dish may be served with pitta bread, a yogurt relish (pages 59–60) and some pickles or salad. It could also be part of a more elaborate meal with meat or chicken, a green vegetable and rice. For speed, I have used canned chick peas which only need 10 minutes of simmering to absorb the flavourings. If you prefer to use dried chick peas, these large, heart-shaped, beige-coloured peas are sold by most supermarkets as well as South Asian and Middle Eastern grocers. Pick over and wash as the packets often include small stones and husks. Whole beans should either be soaked in water overnight before they are cooked or they can be boiled in water for 2 minutes and then left to soak in the boiling water for 1 hour. The cooking time for all pulses varies according to their freshness. The fresher they are, the faster they cook. Store any not used in a tightly lidded container.

Serves 4–5

2 x 500g cans chick peas, drained

4 tbsp vegetable oil

generous pinch of ground asafoetida

1 tsp cumin seeds

175g/6oz onions, chopped

3 garlic cloves, finely chopped

4 tbsp canned chopped tomatoes (See Tip)

2 tsp finely grated fresh root ginger (See Tip, page 24)

300ml/½ pint tea or water

1–2 fresh hot green chillies, cut into very fine rounds (See Tip, page 40)

1 tsp salt

2 tsp ground roasted cumin seeds (See Tip, page 32)

1 tsp shop-bought garam masala

3–4 tbsp coarsely chopped fresh coriander (See Tip, page 39)

1 tbsp fresh lemon juice

1   Rinse the chick peas in fresh water, then drain thoroughly.

2   Heat the oil in a wide pan and when hot, add the asafoetida. Let it sizzle for a second, then add the cumin seeds and let them sizzle for 15 seconds. Add the onions and stir fry until they turn quite brown at the edges, then add the garlic and let it turn golden, stirring continuously.

3   Stir in the tomatoes and cook until they turn dark and thick, then add the ginger, the chick peas and remaining ingredients. Bring to a simmer and cook, uncovered, for 10 minutes stirring, gently, occasionally. Taste and adjust seasoning, if necessary.

Nutrition notes per serving for four: *333 calories, Protein 14g, Carbohydrate 33g, Fat 17g, Saturated fat 1g, Fibre 8g, Added sugar none, Salt 2.20g.*

TIP

If you prefer to use fresh tomatoes, chop finely and use eight tablespoons instead of four. If you want to peel the tomatoes, see Tip, page 48.

Rice

VEGETABLE PULLAO
(SABZI PULLAO) ⓥ

Sometimes when I want an all-vegetarian meal, I serve this with Black-eyed beans with mushrooms (page 48) and a yogurt dish (pages 59–60). It can also be served with any meat.

Serves 6

long grain rice measured to the 450ml/16fl oz level in a glass measuring jug

4 tbsp vegetable oil

1 tsp cumin seeds

115g/4oz potatoes, cut into 5mm/¼in dice

½ medium carrot (about 40g/1½oz), cut into 5mm/¼in dice

40g/1½oz fresh green beans, cut crossways at 5mm/¼in intervals

1¼ tsp salt

½ tsp ground turmeric

1 tsp ground cumin

1 tsp ground coriander

¼ tsp cayenne pepper

½ fresh hot green chilli, finely chopped (See Tip, page 40)

2 tbsp very finely chopped fresh coriander (See Tip, page 39)

½ tsp very finely grated fresh root ginger (See Tip, page 24)

1 garlic clove, mashed to a pulp

1 Place the rice in a bowl and wash in several changes of water until the water runs clear. Drain, add 1.2 litres/2 pints of water and soak for 30 minutes. (See Tip.) Drain and leave in a sieve set over a bowl for 20 minutes.

2 Heat the oil in a heavy pan and when hot, add the cumin seeds and let them sizzle for 5–6 seconds. Add the potatoes, carrot and green beans and stir for 1 minute. Reduce the heat and add the drained rice, salt, turmeric, ground cumin, ground coriander, cayenne, green chilli, coriander, ginger and garlic.

3 Stir the rice for 2–3 minutes, then add 600ml/1 pint water and bring to the boil. Cover very tightly, reduce heat to very low and cook for 25 minutes. Turn off the heat and let the pan sit, covered and undisturbed, for a further 10 minutes.

Nutrition notes per serving: *307 calories, Protein 5g, Carbohydrate 56g, Fat 8g, Saturated fat 1g, Fibre 1g, Added sugar none, Salt 1.02g.*
efore you cook it.

TIP

Washing the rice grains removes the starchy powder left over from the milling process. Put the rice in your largest bowl. Fill the bowl with cold water and gently swirl the rice around it. The water will become cloudy with starch. Carefully pour the water away, holding back the rice with your free hand. Repeat five or six times, or as long as it takes for the water to remain reasonably clear. Soaking the rice lets each grain absorb water so it sticks less to the next grain while cooking. Fill up the bowl again, only this time leave the rice in the water for 20–30 minutes. Draining allows the rice to become fairly dry before you cook it. It should sit in the sieve for at least 20 minutes. If you use this method of preparation, combined with any of the cooking methods in the recipes, you will find that you need dramatically less water than you may have come to expect. Also your rice will have light, separated grains and will taste delicious.

RICE WITH MUSHROOMS AND MUSTARD SEEDS
(KHUMBI CHAAVAL)

Almost any variety of fresh, seasonal mushrooms can be used in this deliciously quick dish. When buying mushrooms look for firm, undamaged specimens. Avoid any that look damp or have been squashed by any wrapping. Mushrooms should never be soaked in water as they absorb it. Many varieties can simply be wiped with a damp cloth. If you do need to wash them, place closed button mushrooms in a colander and rinse well under cold running water. Hold large, flat open mushrooms and cup mushrooms, caps uppermost, under running water and rub gently. Avoid wetting the fins in both cases.

Serves 4–5

long grain rice measured to the 450ml/16fl oz level in a glass measuring jug

3 tbsp vegetable oil

½ tsp cumin seeds

½ tsp black or yellow mustard seeds

25g/1oz onions, cut into fine half-rings

10 medium mushrooms, sliced lengthways

650ml/22fl oz chicken stock or water

½–1 tsp salt

1 Place the rice in a bowl and wash in several changes of water until the water runs clear. (See Tip, page 52.) Drain and leave in a sieve set over a bowl for 20 minutes.

2 Heat the oil in a heavy pan and when hot, add the cumin and mustard seeds. As soon as the mustard seeds begin to pop – this takes just a few seconds – add the onions. Stir fry until the onions brown a little, then add the mushrooms and cook, stirring, for 1 minute.

3 Add the drained rice and stir for 1 minute, then pour in the chicken stock and about half a teaspoon of salt if your stock is salted, one teaspoon if you are using water or unsalted stock. Bring to the boil, cover tightly, then reduce the heat to low and cook for 25 minutes.

Nutrition notes per serving for four: *410 calories, Protein 7g, Carbohydrate 77g, Fat 10g, Saturated fat 1g, Fibre 1g, Added sugar none, Salt 1.19g.*

TIP

If your pan has a loose-fitting lid, cover the pan tightly with foil first, then put on the lid. Crinkle the foil edges so that hardly any steam escapes, if too much does escape the rice will not cook properly. Resist the temptation to peep into a covered pan of rice before the cooking time is over. Precious steam will escape and the rice will cook unevenly. When removing cooked rice from the pan, use a large slotted spoon. Either scrape out the rice gently, layer by layer, or ease the spoon gently into the rice, lift out as much as you can, put it on a plate and then break up any lumps by pressing lightly with the back of the spoon.

RICE WITH PEAS AND DILL (MATAR AUR SOOAY KA PULLAO)

This dish is just as good for the family as it is for dinner guests.

Serves 5–6

basmati rice (See Tip) measured to the 450ml/16fl oz level in a glass measuring jug

3 tbsp vegetable oil

3 whole cloves

4 cardamom pods

1 small onion, cut into fine half-rings

1 tsp salt, plus 1 tsp if using unsalted stock or water

1 tsp Garam masala (page 62)

4 tbsp finely chopped fresh dill or 1½ tbsp dried dill

650ml/22fl oz chicken stock or water

140g/5oz fresh or frozen peas, cooked for 2 minutes in boiling water

1 Place the rice in a bowl and wash well in several changes of water. Drain and leave in a sieve set over a bowl for 20 minutes.

2 Heat the oil in heavy pan and when hot, add the cloves and cardamom pods and stir for a few seconds. Stir in the onion and cook until brown, then add the rice, one teaspoon of salt, the garam masala and dill and stir for 1 minute.

3 Pour in the stock and salt, if necessary and bring to the boil. Cover very tightly, reduce the heat to low and cook for 20 minutes. Add the peas and cook for 5–7 minutes, then stir gently before serving.

Nutrition notes per serving for five: *332 calories, Protein 8g, Carbohydrate 61g, Fat 8g, Saturated fat 1g, Fibre 2g, Added sugar none, Salt 1.42g.*

TIP

Basmati rice grows best in the foothills of the Himalaya mountains, in both India and Pakistan. It is a long grain rice with slender, delicate, naturally-perfumed grains and more expensive than ordinary long grain rice. The best basmati rice is aged for a year before it is sold which inceases its unusual, nutty aroma. It must be picked over, washed and soaked before cooking as it often contains small stones and other impurities.

TURMERIC RICE (PEELAY CHAAVAL) Ⓥ

This yellow, lightly seasoned rice can be served with almost any Indian meal.

Serves 4–6

basmati rice (See Tip) measured to the 450ml/16fl oz level in a glass measuring jug

3 tbsp vegetable oil

3 whole cloves

1 bay leaf

4 cardamom pods

2.5cm/1in cinnamon stick

2 garlic cloves, finely chopped

¼ tsp ground turmeric

1 tsp salt

2 tbsp finely snipped chives or the green part of spring onions, to serve

1 Place the rice in a bowl and wash well in several changes of water. Drain and leave in a sieve set over a bowl for 20 minutes.

2 Heat the oil in heavy pan and when hot, add the cloves, bay leaf, cardamom pods and cinnamon. Stir once or twice, then add the garlic. As soon as the garlic turns brown, add the rice, turmeric and salt. Stir gently for 1 minute.

3 Add 650ml/22fl oz of water and bring to the boil. Cover tightly, reduce the heat to very low and cook for 25 minutes. Just before serving, stir in the chives.

Nutrition notes per serving for four: *375 calories, Protein 7g, Carbohydrate 71g, Fat 9g, Saturated fat 1g, Fibre 1g, Added sugar none, Salt 1.24g.*

Relishes & Chutneys

YOGURT WITH TOMATO AND CUCUMBER

(TIMATAR AUR KHEERAY KA RAITA)

A cooling delight, perfect for hot, spicy meals or eating on its own.

Serves 4-6

450ml/16fl oz natural yogurt

½–¾ tsp salt

freshly ground black pepper

pinch of chilli powder

½ tsp ground roasted cumin seeds (See Tip, page 32)

1 small tomato, cut into small dice

10cm/4in piece cucumber, peeled and cut into small dice

1 Beat the yogurt lightly with a fork until smooth, then add remaining ingredients and mix well.

Nutrition notes per serving for four: *67 calories, Protein 6g, Carbohydrate 8g, Fat 1g, Saturated fat 1g, Fibre 1g, Added sugar none, Salt 0.85g.*

FRESH RED CHUTNEY WITH ALMONDS

(LAL CHUTNEY)

For a hotter chutney substitute fresh, hot red chillies in place of the red pepper and chilli powder. If you prefer, use walnuts instead of almonds. Both are traditional and authentic. This will keep in the fridge for a few days.

Serves 8

85g/3oz red pepper, seeded and coarsely chopped

20 large mint leaves, coarsely chopped

2 tbsp fresh lemon juice

1 garlic clove, coarsely chopped

½ tsp chilli powder

½ tsp salt

freshly ground black pepper

1 tbsp blanched, chopped or slivered almonds

1 tsp chopped fresh dill (optional)

1 Place all the ingredients, except the almonds and dill, in a blender and process until smooth. Add the almonds and briefly process again. Transfer to a serving bowl, check seasoning and stir in the dill, if using.

Nutrition notes per serving for four: *18 calories, Protein 1g, Carbohydrate 1g, Fat 1g, Saturated fat trace, Fibre 1g, Added sugar none, Salt 0.32g.*

FRESH GREEN CHUTNEY

(HARI CHUTNEY)

This can be served with all Indian meals. It can be stored, covered, in the fridge for two to three days.

Serves 6

6 tbsp natural yogurt

2 heaped tbsp coarsely chopped fresh mint

2 heaped tbsp coarsely chopped fresh coriander (See Tip, page 39)

1 tbsp fresh lemon juice

pinch of salt or to taste

1 Place two tablespoons of the yogurt, the mint, coriander, lemon juice and salt in a blender and process until smooth.

2 Place the remaining yogurt in a bowl and beat lightly. Add the paste from the blender and stir to mix.

Nutrition notes per serving: *11 calories, Protein 1g, Carbohydrate 1g, Fat 1g, Saturated fat trace, Fibre none, Added sugar none, Salt 0.36g.*

YOGURT WITH CARROT AND SULTANAS

(GAJAR AUR KISHMISH KA RAITA)

This can also be served at the end of a meal as a salad-cum-dessert.

Serves 4

300ml/½ pint natural yogurt

½ tsp sugar

¼ tsp salt

¼ tsp chilli powder

1 medium carrot, coarsely grated

1 tbsp vegetable oil

¼ tsp cumin seeds

¼ tsp black or yellow mustard seeds

2 tbsp sultanas

1 Beat the yogurt lightly with a fork until smooth and creamy, then add the sugar, salt, chilli powder and carrot and mix together.
2 Heat the oil in a small frying pan and when very hot, add the cumin and mustard seeds. As soon as the mustard seeds begin to pop – this takes just a few seconds – put in the sultanas. Stir once, then empty into the bowl of yogurt and mix together well.

Nutrition notes per serving:
95 calories, Protein 4g, Carbohydrate 12g, Fat 4g, Saturated fat 1g, Fibre 1g, Added sugar 1g, Salt 0.41g.

TOMATO, ONION AND CORIANDER RELISH

(CACHUMBER)

This tasty relish complements almost all Indian meals.

Serve 4–6

225g/8oz tomatoes, cut into 5mm/¼ in dice

85g/3oz onions, cut into 5mm/¼ in dice

4 heaped tbsp chopped fresh coriander (See Tip, page 39)

¾ tsp salt

2 tbsp fresh lemon juice

½ tsp cayenne pepper

½ tsp ground, roasted cumin seeds (See Tip, page 32)

1 Place all the ingredients in a non-metallic serving bowl and mix together.

Nutrition notes per serving for four: *25 calories, Protein 1g, Carbohydrate 4g, Fat 1g, Saturated fat trace, Fibre 1g, Added sugar none, Salt 1.01g.*

ONION RELISH

(PYAZ KA LACCHA)

This may be familiar to you from Indian restaurants where it is sometimes described as onion chutney. It can be served with almost every Indian meal.

Serves 4

115g/4oz onions, cut crossways into paper thin rings

¾ tsp salt

4 tsp fresh lemon juice

¼ tsp paprika (the redder in colour, the better)

pinch of cayenne pepper

1 Place all the ingredients in a bowl, toss together and set aside for 30 minutes or more before eating to allow the flavours to blend.

Nutrition notes per serving:
12 calories, Protein 1g, Carbohydrate 3g, Fat trace, Saturated fat trace, Fibre 1g, Added sugar none, Salt 0.99g.

Basic Recipes

GARAM MASALA

This aromatic mixture generally incorporates spices that are supposed to heat the body (the words mean 'hot spices') such as large black cardamoms, cinnamon, black cumin (also called *shah zeera* or royal cumin), cloves, black peppercorns and nutmeg. It is used sparingly and generally added to foods towards the end of cooking time. It is also used as a garnish.

This recipe is one of my favourites. It is best to grind this in small quantities so that it stays fresh. When a recipe calls for shop-bought do not substitute my recipe, even if you have some. The tastes are quite different.

Makes 3 tablespoons

1 tbsp green cardamom seeds
5cm/2in cinnamon stick
1 tsp cumin seeds
1 tsp whole cloves
1 tsp black peppercorns
¼ of an average size nutmeg

1 Place all the ingredients in a clean coffee grinder or spice grinder. Turn the machine on for 30–40 seconds or until the spices are finely ground. Store in a small jar with a tight-fitting lid.

GHEE

Not all Indian food is cooked in ghee. I feel that cooking in ghee is like cooking in butter – it is fine some of the time for selected dishes. Many of our foods are meant to be cooked in vegetable oil. Ghee is butter that has been clarified so thoroughly that you can even deep-fry in it. No milk solids are left in and it does not need to be kept in the fridge. It has a nutty, buttery taste.

You can buy ghee ready-made from Asian grocers. If you wish to make it yourself you can.

450g/1lb unsalted butter

1 Melt the butter in a small, heavy pan over a low heat. Simmer very gently for 10–30 minutes. The length of time will depend upon the amount of water in the butter. As soon as the white milky residue turns to golden particles (you have to keep watching), strain the ghee through several layers of cheesecloth or a handkerchief. Cool, pour into a clean jar and cover. Properly made it does not need to be chilled.

TARKA

I do not know of this technique being used anywhere else in the world. Oil or ghee is heated until very hot (but not burning), then spices, generally whole ones, or chopped up garlic and ginger, are added to the oil. The seasonings swell, brown, pop or otherwise change character.

This seasoned oil, together with all the spices is then poured over cooked foods such as pulses and vegetables or uncooked foods are added to it, then sautéed or simmered.

The most commonly used seasonings include whole cumin seeds, whole black mustard seeds, whole fennel seeds, whole dried red chillies, whole cloves, cinnamon sticks, cardamom pods, bay leaves and black peppercorns.

These seasonings are not meant to be eaten but are left to one side of the plate along with any bones.

INDEX